j970.1
L96o

P9-DOE-048

3 5674 02088876 0

DETROIT PUBLIC LIBRARY
CHASE BRANCH LIBRARY
17731 W. Seven Mile Rd.
Detroit, MI 48235
935-5346
DATE DUE

OCT 1 0 1994

OCT 1 8 1995

APR 1 8 1996

DEC 01 1996

SEP 2 1 1998

DEC 0 1 1998

OCT 0 5 1999

JUL 1 0 2000

JUL 2 '94

C.H

The OJIBWAS
People of the Northern Forests

BY EILEEN LUCAS

NATIVE AMERICANS
THE MILLBROOK PRESS
BROOKFIELD, CONNECTICUT

To Gail Pachuki for all her help in
getting me started and keeping me going.

Migwetch!

Cover photo courtesy of the American Museum of Natural History
Trans. No. 3745, Photo by Kerry Perkins
Photos courtesy of the National Museum of American Art,
Washington, D.C./Art Resource: p. 10; New York Public
Library Picture Collection: pp. 13, 21, 51 (top); Milwaukee
Public Museum: pp. 14, 51 (bottom); American Museum of Natural
History: pp. 15, (R. Wanamaker, neg. no. 316346), 22 (Richard
P. Sheridan, neg. no. 2A 12858), 24 (neg. no. 115961); James
Jerome Hill Reference Library: p. 19; National Museum of the
American Indian, Smithsonian Institution: p. 25 (neg. no.
33721); The Capitol, Washington, D.C.: pp. 28, 31; Bettmann:
pp. 35, 39, 52; Minnesota Historical Society: pp. 42 (photo:
Hoard & Tenney), 44 (photo: James S. Drysdale), 47.
Maps by Joe Le Monnier

Library of Congress Cataloging-in-Publication Data
Lucas, Eileen.
The Ojibwas : people of the northern forests / by Eileen Lucas.
p.   cm.
Includes bibliographical references and index.
ISBN 1-56294-313-8 (lib. bdg.)
1. Ojibwa Indians—Juvenile literature.   I. Title.
E99.C6L78 1994 973'.04973—dc20 93-18640 CIP

Published by The Millbrook Press
2 Old New Milford Road, Brookfield, Connecticut 06804

Copyright © 1994 by Eileen Lucas
All rights reserved
Printed in the United States of America
1   3   5   6   4   2

CONTENTS

The
Ojibwas

OJIBWA LANDS

FACTS ABOUT
THE TRADITIONAL OJIBWA
WAY OF LIFE

GROUP NAME:

Ojibwa or Chippewa
Call themselves Anishinabe, "Original People"

MAJOR CLANS:

Crane, Fish, Loon, Bear,
Martin, Deer, and Bird

LANGUAGE:

Algonquian family

HOUSE TYPE:

Birchbark wigwam

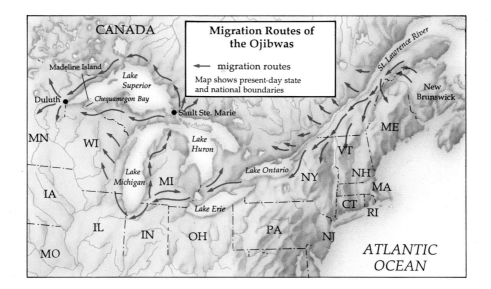

GEOGRAPHIC REGION:

Between the years 1000 and 1400, migrated
from the northern Atlantic coast, around the
mouth of the St. Lawrence River, to the eastern
shores of Lake Superior. Their homeland
became all the land around the Lake Superior
area, reaching westward into Minnesota
and the Dakotas, southward into Wisconsin
and Michigan, and northward into Canada.

MAIN FOODS:

Berries, nuts, leeks, corn, squash,
wild potatoes, wild rice, maple sugar,
large and small game, and fish.

Chapter One

ANISHINABE STORIES

By the flickering firelight on a winter's night, a group of people gather to hear the stories of the elders. Young children and their parents sit quietly while the old ones speak. Even the babies seem to listen to the beautiful sounds of the words.

A grandfather tells of how these people's ancestors left their homes along the Atlantic shores of the St. Lawrence River, in southeastern Canada, a long, long time ago. They followed the Great River west toward the setting sun. Sometimes they stopped to set up villages along the way. A season or two—or many years—might pass before they would move on. But always the spirits told them when the time was right to continue the journey.

The ancestors called themselves *Anishinabe*, "Original People." Their neighbors called them Ojibwas. Some people think that this word meant "picture-makers," because of the *picto-*

The pictographs on the clothing of this
Ojibwa chief illustrate his many exploits.

graphs (stories told in pictures) that the Anishinabe made. Others say that it was a word for the puckered seams that made their moccasins unusual. Later the Europeans would call them Chippewas, a name that is still often used today.

THE NEW HOMELAND ▪ After many generations, the people came at last to the shores of Kitchi Gami, now called Lake Superior. This largest of the Great Lakes would become the heart of the new homeland.

The stories tell that the Ojibwas had settled along the shores of Lake Superior by the 1400s. Throughout the following centuries, they spread out north, south, east, and west from there, searching for the best winter hunting grounds and the best summer village sites.

The Ojibwas found that this new homeland was rich in natural resources. The forests supplied materials for their houses and canoes and were home to animals that provided food and clothing. There were bears and moose, elk and deer, as well as smaller game like wolves, coyotes, foxes, and rabbits. There were also the creatures of the water—beavers, otters, muskrats, and fishes. There were birds, such as ducks, pheasants, and turkeys. There were wild berries, nuts, roots, and wild vegetables to add to the crops the people grew.

The Ojibwas lived mostly in small villages and campsites scattered throughout the northern woods, but they had a unique tribal identity and a rich culture that held them together. They lived in harmony with their environment, believing that there were spirits in all the things of nature, and that all living beings were equals in the circle of life. This was what the stories of the elders told them.

Chapter Two

WAYS OF
THE WIGWAM

The Ojibwa people developed a culture that was a mixture of old ways brought with them on the great journey and new ways learned in the new homeland. Daily life in these early times was filled with the work of obtaining and preparing food and the crafting of tools for survival.

COMMUNITY LIFE ▪ In an Ojibwa community there were jobs for men, women, and children, and more than enough work to keep everyone busy. The individuals of a community learned to work together for the good of the whole community. For example, men were generally the hunters, killing the animals that would be used for food and clothing. Women cooked the food and prepared and sewed the animal hides.

The home of the Ojibwas was called a wigwam. Men cut the saplings that would make up the wigwam's framework. These

The northern woods, with its many rivers and lakes and lush natural resources, proved to be the perfect settling place for the early Ojibwas.

This 1933 photograph of Ojibwa wigwams shows how they were placed close together in small communities. Each wigwam housed one extended family, but all the families gardened and hunted together to provide for the whole group.

saplings were placed in the ground in a circle, and then bound together at the top in a series of arches. Several poles were tied to the saplings horizontally around the circle. Mats of woven grasses and large strips of birchbark were then laid over this framework. Heavy poles were sometimes laid over the mats and bark to keep them in place. A hole was left in the center of the roof for smoke to escape, and the doorway was covered with a piece of animal skin. Using previously stored pieces of bark and mats, the Ojibwas could construct a sturdy wigwam in less than a day.

Inside the wigwam a low fire burned in the central firepit. Around the inside edges of the wigwam were low benches and mats for sleeping and sitting, and baskets containing the family's belongings. Each wigwam usually housed a family made up of grandparents, parents, and several children.

Ojibwa babies spent most of their first year of life strapped to a cradleboard. A flat board was used for this, with a footrest at the bottom and a hoop to protect the baby's head at the top. The baby was placed on a layer of moss and feathers laid on the board. A piece of animal hide or fur covered the baby, and a strip of leather wrapped around the cradleboard held the baby in place. In a cradleboard a baby could be carried long distances on its mother's back and propped safely against a wigwam or a tree while the mother worked.

A late nineteenth-century photograph captures an Ojibwa baby staring serenely out at the world from the security of its cradleboard. The mother is probably resting from her work in the fields.

After children outgrew the cradleboard, they began the process of finding their place in the family and community. In their games and chores, boys and girls learned the skills they would need later in life. When a boy made his first animal kill, his parents held a celebration because he was learning to provide food for his family. When he was old enough, he was encouraged to go on a Vision Quest. This meant spending several days alone in the woods without food or water so that his guardian spirit could speak to him and direct him in his life. When a girl reached *puberty* (around the age of twelve), she was welcomed into the community of women and she prepared to take on the work of being a wife and mother.

The Ojibwas believed that when a person died he or she passed into the spirit world. Food and other things that were important to that person (such as weapons for a man, perhaps a cooking pot or needle and thread for a woman) were buried with the body. These would be useful to the spirit of the person while it made its four-day journey to the spirit world. Sometimes small buildings were constructed over the grave to provide shelter for the spirits.

CLAN AND KINSHIP ▪ Because the Ojibwas traditionally lived in scattered villages, there have always been many separate groups, called bands, within the Ojibwa tribe. Each small community had its own leaders, and most decisions, even whether or not to join in a war, were made separately by the community.

Even though there was little governmental connection between bands of Ojibwas, other ties held them together as a people. One of these ties was the clan and kinship system. Among the Ojibwas a clan was a group of people related through their fathers.

The Ojibwas placed great importance on the clan a person was born into. An individual considered all members of the clan to be his relatives, and marriage between members of a clan was forbidden.

The major Ojibwa clans were the Crane, Fish, Loon, Bear, Martin, Deer, and Bird. (Since the early days, more clans have been added.) Each clan had certain responsibilities to the community. For example, members of the Fish clan were often given the responsibility of resolving differences between other clans.

RELIGIOUS BELIEFS ▪ The Ojibwas did not separate religion from other aspects of life. The things they believed in affected everything they did.

One of their most basic beliefs was that all living creatures were equally important in the circle of life. Another was that all the things of nature—trees and rivers and rocks, as well as animals—were occupied by a *manido*, or spirit.

There were many lesser spirits and greater spirits, some of whom were evil, although most were good. There was one Great Spirit, Kitchi Manido, who was especially respected, and no one would say his name except with great reverence. He created Winebozho, First Man (also called Nanabush) and from First Man came the Anishinabe.

Persons who took care to please the spirits would stay healthy and be successful in the things they did. Those who angered the spirits would have bad luck; they might even get sick and die.

One of the best ways to please the spirits was with the offering of tobacco, the gift of thanksgiving. Each time an animal was killed, an offering was made to the spirit of the animal, thanking it for giving up its life. Before the wild rice was harvested, and before large strips of birchbark were peeled from trees, an offering of tobacco was made. Throughout the seasons of the year offerings were made to the spirits, in order that their good fortune might continue.

When the Ojibwas were not in good health they had several kinds of medicine men to turn to. Most medicine men were a combination of priest and doctor. The Ojibwas believed that good relations with the spirits and good health were closely related. The medicine men were usually people considered to have a special relationship with the spirit world.

Many of the medicine men of the Ojibwas were members of a special medicine society known as the *Midewiwin*. Members of the Midewiwin combined a knowledge of herbs and physical healing with their special relationship with the spirits to help promote good health among the Ojibwas. Members of the Midewiwin believed that right living—following the wishes of good spirits and avoiding evil ones—and proper use of plants and herbs would lead to long life. Each member carried a medicine bag that held things that would bring good health. Midewiwin ceremonies were times of sacred song and dance and prayer.

Sacred songs and dances were important in Ojibwa life. The Ojibwas were known as a people who loved to sing. They also used musical instruments, including drums, rattles, and flutes. The rhythm and words of songs and the steps and motions of dances were symbolic and meaningful to the people.

A medicine man prays to the spirits to cure his patient. Members of the Midewiwin, a healing society, used plants and herbs to treat the sick.

CRAFTS AND CLOTHING ▪ There was great symbolism and meaning in the things that the Ojibwas made too, things that we might call crafts. These items were often formed and decorated in a way that told something special about the person making them, or about the person who would use them.

These crafts were all made from the things of nature. Dyes were made from roots, nuts, bark, and berries. Baskets were made from roots, twigs, bark, grass, and reeds. Mats were woven from the cattails, rushes, and reeds that grew in the swampy land around many of the lakes in Ojibwa territory.

Clothing was made from the hides of animals, mostly deer. Men and boys wore a breechcloth, a strip of hide that passed between the legs and over a belt to hang down in front and back. Leggings that came up to the thighs were attached to the belt by a leather thong. In cold weather a warm fur or animal skin would be wrapped around the man's shoulders.

Women and girls wore a dress made by sewing two pieces of deerskin together at the shoulders and down the sides. Women usually wore knee-high leggings tied at the knees with a leather band. Children's clothes were similar to adults', but were often made from smaller skins or furs such as beaver, fawn, squirrel, or rabbit. All the Ojibwas wore leather moccasins with soft soles to allow them to move quietly in the forest.

For personal decoration, both men and women oiled and braided their hair. Sometimes they stuck feathers and porcupine quills in their hair. They also painted their faces, wore earrings, necklaces, and bracelets, and often decorated their clothing with beautiful designs in quills, feathers, and beadwork.

The style of dress for Ojibwa women was quite elaborate, as shown in this 1857 painting by Eastman Johnson. Rich dyes made from plants and berries were used to color the deerskin and cloth.

An Ojibwa doll decorated with beadwork.

The Ojibwas and other Native Americans were very clever in finding items to use as beads. Shells, stones, animal teeth, claws, and hooves—even nuts, berries, and seeds—were strung together and attached to other things for decoration. When Europeans began trading glass beads to the Indians for furs, Ojibwa women became quite skilled in fancy beadwork.

The Ojibwas used the trees of the northern forests in many ways. A flat piece of wood such as ash or hickory was used in making a bow. Slender shoots of trees were used for arrows, with sharpened bits of bone or flint for arrowheads.

The inner bark of cedar trees was dried and crushed and used as body powder. Fibers from the inner barks of certain trees made an excellent string for fishing and hunting snares.

For snowshoes a piece of pliable (flexible) wood was bent and held in place with strips of hide. Animal sinews and twine made from the inner bark of trees made a netting to hold the foot in place on the snowshoe. Snowshoes allowed the Ojibwas to travel and hunt in deep winter snows.

One of the most important resources for Ojibwa crafts was the bark of the birch tree. Birchbark was plentiful in Ojibwa territory and was used to make many things, including torches, dishes, buckets, and canoes, and also to cover wigwams. Birchbark containers, called *makuks*, were used to store rice, maple syrup, sugar, corn, and berries. When sealed with *pitch*, birchbark containers could even hold water.

The Ojibwas were masters of the art of making birchbark canoes. The birchbark canoe was light, which made it easy to *portage* (carry) over land and fast in the water. At the same time it was strong enough to carry heavy loads of people and goods. The ends of the canoe were pointed to make steering through rough waters easier.

GAMES ▪ The Ojibwa way of life involved a lot of work, but there was time for play as well. The Ojibwas enjoyed many games of skill and chance. Their culture was rich in humor and fun. They loved to tell jokes and poke fun at one another and at outsiders. They told stories for enjoyment as well as for learning, and sang during special ceremonies as well as for pleasure.

Most Native American tribes played a form of ball game, and the Ojibwas were no exception. The men played a rough, fast-moving game that the French named lacrosse. Each player held one stick with a small hoop at one end. This stick was used to propel a small ball toward and over the other team's goalpost. Games often took a full day to play. There were often several dozen players on each team, and games sometimes got quite rough. Players were expected to accept injury and pain without getting angry or taking it personally.

The Ojibwa women had their own games, including one like field hockey called shinny. Shinny players used a curved stick to drive the ball forward along the ground. They also played a variation of lacrosse called double-ball, in which two balls were tied together.

Birchbark Art

Sometimes Ojibwa women decorated birchbark containers by painting on them using birchbark stencils. This is something you can try for yourself. If you can't find any birchbark where you live, you can make a similar stencil with some stiff cardboard.

To make the stencil, draw a shape on the piece of bark or cardboard. For example, you can draw the outline of the sun, or of a dog, bird, or other animal. Then carefully cut out the inside of the shape with a scissors or knife. (Be sure to have an adult help you with this.) When your stencil is ready, place it over another piece of birchbark or other item to be decorated. Spread paint or ink over the cutout portion of the stencil. Carefully lift the stencil away and you'll see the decoration you have made.

Birchbark containers with stenciled designs.

*An 1861 painting by George Catlin shows
three young men posing in ball-play dress
and paint. Each was chosen as the best lacrosse
player from his tribe. From left to right are
a Choctaw, an Ojibwa, and a Sioux.*

Among the children one of the favorite games was snow snake. The players threw a long stick representing a snake along a frozen path in the snow competing to see who could throw the stick the farthest. Snake sticks were usually about 6 feet (183 centimeters) long, with a knob on one end to represent the head. Snake sticks were polished, oiled, and decorated by young players.

Chapter Three

A CULTURE FOR ALL SEASONS

The climate of the northern Great Lakes area where the Ojibwas settled can be described as subarctic, with long, cold, snowy winters and short summers. Each season provided the Ojibwas with different kinds of foods, and this wide variety made for a nutritious, well-balanced diet.

SPRING MOONS ▪ Spring began with Crust on the Snow Moon (March). Mild days followed by freezing nights meant that the sap began to run in the maple trees. The Ojibwas moved from their winter hunting grounds to the maple sugar groves. Several families gathered in each camp to help each other with the work of maple sugar production.

Small spouts of wood were driven into the trees, and birchbark baskets were set underneath. Every day the sap that dripped into the baskets was added to a large pot, where it was boiled until it thickened into syrup. Some syrup was dropped onto the snow to cool and be eaten like candy, and some was stored for later use. Most of it was transferred into smaller pots where it was stirred with a paddle until it separated into grains of maple sugar. This sugar was the primary seasoning of the Ojibwas. They used it on fruits and in stews, and even as a seasoning for meats and fish.

This work went on through the Moon of Boiling Sap (April), until the arrival of Flowering Moon (May), when the Ojibwas prepared to move to their summer camp.

SUMMER MOONS ▪ With the coming of Strawberry Moon (June), larger groups of families gathered in summer villages to grow and gather food. Through this month and the two that followed, Midsummer Moon (July) and Blueberry Moon (August), the fields were ripe with many kinds of wild plants. There were potatoes and other root vegetables. There were greens like leeks and onions that added flavor to soups and stews. There were many kinds of berries that could be eaten fresh, dried, or boiled in maple sugar. Hot and cold drinks were made from leaves (such as wintergreen), fruits (such as chokecherries), and roots (such as swamproot).

The Ojibwas made use of the short growing season as best they could. They grew corn, squash, turnips, and pumpkins. The corn was often picked while still green since summer usually ended before it was completely ripe. Some was eaten when harvested, either boiled or roasted on the cob. Some was saved for next year's crop. Most was dried and stored for winter use. This dried corn could then be added to soups or stews or ground into a kind of flour for use in bread.

Chippewa (Ojibwa) women harvesting wild rice.
Because the rice grows in water several feet deep,
canoes provide the best means for gathering.

AUTUMN MOONS ▪ As summer ended and Wild Rice Moon (September) approached, it was time to move to the shores of the lakes where the wild rice grew. This wild rice (actually, a wild grass) was an important part of the Ojibwa diet. It was usually harvested by three people in a canoe. One poled the canoe gently through the watery fields of rice while the others sat in the canoe with two sticks or paddles. One stick was used to bend the tops of the stalks over the canoe. The other was used to knock the grains of rice off into the bottom of the canoe. Some of the grains fell into the water, seeding next year's crop.

Then the rice was parched, or dried, in a large pot over a fire. It had to be stirred constantly so that it dried without burning. Then it was threshed—that is, the husk was removed from the

Wild Rice

Wild rice was harvested in the fall. Because it could be stored and eaten during the winter when other types of food were scarce, it was an important food for the Ojibwas.

To make your own wild rice dish, start by bringing two cups of water to a boil. Add one cup of wild rice (available in most supermarkets) to the pot. You should use two to three times as much water as rice. Cover the pot and reduce the heat so that the water just simmers gently. Cook for about thirty minutes, until the rice is chewy but not mushy.

There are a number of things you can add to the rice for flavor. The Ojibwas used maple sugar or maple syrup for seasoning. Add about one tablespoon to one pot of rice. You may also add chopped onion, boiled corn, or pine nuts. Wild rice is also very good with slivered almonds that have been lightly toasted in a warm oven (about 250 degrees Fahrenheit, or 130 degrees Celsius) for about ten minutes.

kernel of rice. This was done by putting the rice in a sack and beating the sack with a club, or by placing the rice in a hole in the ground lined with hide and dancing on it.

The last step was winnowing the rice. This involved putting the rice on bark trays and gently shaking the trays so that the loosened husks blew away in the wind, leaving the grains of rice to be cooked and eaten or stored for winter use.

After the wild rice was gathered, Falling Leaves Moon (October) arrived and additional preparations were made for the long cold months of winter.

WINTER MOONS ▪ By the time Freezing Moon (November) arrived, families had headed for the winter hunting grounds. Often there were only one or two other families within a day's walking distance. The women had many winter jobs to do, such as repairing clothes and making baskets. The men hunted ducks and geese and other game. While hunting and fishing were carried on throughout the year, they were essential in winter, when eating animals and fish kept the Ojibwas from starving.

The Ojibwas hunted and trapped many kinds of wild animals. Traditionally, they hunted with bow and arrow, spear, and knives. They also used many kinds of traps, such as a large *deadfall* trap made out of logs, to capture and kill animals without damaging the hide or fur. Rabbits and smaller animals were caught in *snares*.

Fishing has always been an important part of the Ojibwa culture. The homeland of the Ojibwas is covered with lakes and rivers filled with fish. The Ojibwas were skilled in catching them, especially through holes in the ice during the cold of winter. Trout, sturgeon, and muskie were among their favorites.

The Ojibwas have long been known as
accomplished spearfishermen. In the winter
they set up camps along the frozen rivers and
lakes and fish through holes chopped in the ice.

■ 31 ■

With the coming of Spirit Moon (December), winter was well under way. During this and the next two months, Great Spirit Moon (January) and Sucker Fish Moon (February), the family relied on food the women had stored and on fresh fish and meat brought in by the men. Often they were hungry. Nights were spent by the fire, listening to stories told by the elders—and waiting for spring to come again.

Chapter Four

TIMES OF CHANGE

About a thousand years ago the Ojibwas were one of many tribes that spoke an Algonquian language, had similar customs, and lived in the woods of northeastern North America. When they began to migrate westward away from the mouth of the St. Lawrence River, they were accompanied by two other tribes, the Ottawas and the Potawatomis. Together they were known as the Three Fires Council.

When they reached the shores of Lake Huron, the people of the Three Fires split up. The Ottawas settled along the northern shores of Lake Huron. The Potawatomis moved into the area that is now Michigan.

The Ojibwas continued northwest to the shores of Lake Superior. They established villages at several places along Superior's shores. One of the most important villages was Bowating (where Sault Sainte Marie is today). Another was on Madeline Island in the sheltered bay called Chequamegon.

Throughout the following centuries, as the Ojibwas explored their new territory, they encountered other groups of Native Americans. Some, like their old friends the Ottawas, and the Hurons, became trading partners. Others, like the Five Nations of the Iroquois Confederacy, became fierce enemies.

THE FUR TRADE ■ As the Ojibwas traded and visited with other Indians, they learned of a people from a far-off land who had arrived in the east. It seemed that these fair-skinned strangers were very interested in obtaining the furs of animals that the Indians were skilled in hunting. In return for these furs, they offered marvelous pots and needles and knives of iron, and shooting sticks that could kill animals and enemies more effectively than bows and arrows.

Several Indian tribes began acting as middlemen between these Europeans on the eastern coast and Indians who lived farther inland. Long before the French actually set foot in Ojibwa camps, the Ojibwas were trading furs with their neighbors for European goods.

The development of the fur trade was to have an enormous effect on the cultures of the *indigenous* (native) peoples of North America. For the first time Native Americans began hunting animals as a business, rather than just for their own use.

One result of this was that they gradually became dependent on the trade goods they received for the furs, and became less skilled in making things the traditional ways. They started living in permanent villages near trading centers instead of moving from place to place in search of food. The animals that had been a primary source of food became scarce.

*By the mid-seventeenth century, fur-trading
was brisk between the French and the Indians.
While the hunting skills of the Indians allowed
the trading companies to prosper, the Indians
benefited less than the French.*

Another effect of the fur trade was an increase in warfare.
The European nations involved (primarily France and England)
struggled for control of the trade routes. There was warfare between Indian tribes over the use of hunting grounds. Since fighting was now being done with guns rather than the traditional
bows and arrows, the number of Indians that died from warfare
increased dramatically. Added to this was the introduction of
European diseases, which killed many thousands of Native
Americans.

MISSIONARIES AND TRADERS ▪ As time went on, French traders became interested in visiting the interior of the continent. Following the trade routes long used by the Indians, they began to bring their trade goods, and their way of life, to the Ojibwas.

The first contact between the Ojibwas and the Europeans was probably at a feast at a Huron camp in September 1641. Several Ojibwas were guests of the Hurons at this feast, as were several French missionaries (people who were trained to spread the teachings of Christianity).

A few weeks later, two French missionaries, Father Charles Raymbault and Father Isaac Jogues, arrived at the Ojibwa village of Bowating. They called this place Sault Sainte Marie (Saint Mary's Rapids) and the people Saulteurs (People of the Rapids).

These missionaries were soon followed by others. They usually found that the Ojibwas were satisfied with their own religion. The Ojibwas were less interested in Christianity than in the European trade goods that French explorers and traders brought.

In 1659 two French traders, Pierre Esprit Radisson and Medard Chouart des Groseilliers, traveled by canoe from the French trading post at Quebec to Lake Superior. They visited many Ojibwa camps during the winter, exchanging goods for furs. When they returned the following spring to Quebec, their boats were loaded with furs. This convinced other traders that the Lake Superior area was worth visiting. Soon the Ojibwa village at Chequamegon Bay became a trading center where Ojibwas and other Indians brought furs to exchange for French trade goods.

The French trappers and traders who were soon traveling throughout Ojibwa territory became an important part of Ojibwa social, economic, and political life. Many of them married Ojibwa women and lived at least part of the time in native villages. They learned the Ojibwa language and customs, and adopted many of the Indians' ways, including the use of deerskin clothing and birchbark canoes. They came to be known as *voyageurs* for the long journeys they made along the trade routes. Some were called *coureurs de bois* ("runners of the woods"). These were the independent, unlicensed traders who lived a dangerous life in search of adventure and wealth in the fur trade.

EXPANDING TERRITORY ■ By the late 1600s the Ojibwas were spreading out over an increasingly large territory. Some bands moved eastward along the north shore of Lake Huron and as far east as Lake Ontario, fighting with Iroquois for control of this territory. These Ojibwas were sometimes called Mississauga Ojibwas. Their villages centered in what is now the Toronto area.

At the same time, some bands of Ojibwas moved southward from the shores of Lake Superior into what is now Wisconsin, forcing the Fox who lived there to move farther south. Some Ojibwas also moved westward from the tip of Lake Superior into the eastern Minnesota area, sometimes fighting with the Sioux for control of this territory.

By this time the British had an active fur trade going to the north along Hudson Bay and to the southeast in the New York area. The French did not want the Ojibwas and their neighbors trading with the British. They gave the Indians around Sault Sainte Marie many gifts and asked them to trade only with

French traders. In 1679 a Frenchman named Daniel Greysolon Duluth spoke to the Indians at the western end of Lake Superior, including Ojibwas and Sioux, asking them to make peace with each other and to become French allies.

For the next decade or two business was good in the fur trade in the Lake Superior region. But when the French government decided there were too many furs on the market, they temporarily stopped buying from the Indians.

With the fur trade gone, the Ojibwas had no way to support themselves. When the French returned to Madeline Island to reopen trading in 1718, they found that the Indians in the area were close to starving. Conditions improved a little as the fur trade became active in Ojibwa territory again.

WAR IN THE LAND OF LAKES ▪ Since the treaty with Duluth in 1679, the Sioux and the Ojibwas at the west end of Lake Superior had been trading partners with the French. When the Sioux attacked French outposts in 1736, they and the Ojibwas became enemies again. Fighting spread throughout the upper Mississippi River valley and as far west as the Dakotas.

Most of the fighting was done in quick attacks by raiding parties rather than large battles. The Ojibwas were often victorious for several reasons. They usually were better equipped with European weapons than the Sioux, and they were among the best woodsmen of all the Indians. Their superior birchbark canoes were also a great advantage. Slowly the Ojibwas forced the Sioux to move westward out of Wisconsin and away from northeastern Minnesota.

At the same time that the Ojibwas and their neighbors were

In this painting of a scene from the French and Indian War, a soldier attacks an Indian from behind. After the French lost the war, the Ojibwas had to learn to deal with the British who took control of the Great Lakes fur trade.

fighting for control of hunting grounds, the French and the British were fighting for colonial control of North America.

The Ojibwas and other Algonquian-speaking tribes tended to side with the French, while their enemies the Iroquois were allies of the British. When the British won the French and Indian War in 1763, the French pulled their soldiers from North America. The British then took control of the Great Lakes fur trade.

Many of the Great Lakes Indians preferred the old arrangement with the French. Many Frenchmen had married Indian women and lived in Indian villages as brothers. They were interested primarily in the business of the fur trade, while British settlers were interested in owning Indian land.

Some bands of Ojibwas joined in an uprising led by the Ottawa chief Pontiac. Pontiac hoped that French soldiers and traders would return to North America to help the Indians defeat the British. When he realized that the French government was gone for good, he decided that his people would have to accept the British presence, and the rebellion came to an end.

From the mid-1760s through the 1770s the Ojibwas traded peacefully with the British. When the American colonies revolted against British rule, the Ojibwas remained neutral. But when the British lost the war, control of the Great Lakes fur trade was given to the Americans. The Americans further increased their control by defeating the British in the War of 1812. Now the Ojibwas were supposed to trade with Americans, whose goods were often inferior to those of the Europeans and whose settlers were increasingly land-hungry.

Some Ojibwas moved into Canadian territory so that they could trade with the British. American influence in Ojibwa territory that was now claimed by the United States increased.

A CHANGING WAY OF LIFE ▪ In the United States in the 1820s and 1830s, the fur trade was run primarily by the American Fur Company, owned by John Jacob Astor. This company had several outposts in Ojibwa territory and was interested in maintaining the wilderness and Indian culture for the benefit of the fur trade.

There were others with a very different point of view, however. Settlers, lumbermen, and miners were coming to the Great Lakes area in larger numbers. They wanted to change the face of the land, and in order to do this they wanted to move the Indians out.

Throughout the 1830s there was increasing pressure on the Great Lakes Indians to move westward across the Mississippi. This was part of the government's "removal" policy. In both Canada and the United States, tens of thousands of Indian people were forced to move to special lands "reserved" for them.

The Ojibwas did not want to part with their maple sugar groves, their rice lakes, or their birchwood forests. They did not want to leave the burial grounds of their ancestors. They insisted that they had allowed the French, British, and Americans to use the land but had never given up their right to live there and use it as well.

Reservations were established for the Ojibwas within their tribal territories in both the United States and Canada. Slowly, the majority of the Ojibwa people gathered at these sites.

Each reservation came to reflect the uniqueness of the band that lived there and the conditions of its environment. Each struggled to survive in this new world, a world very different from that of the Ojibwa ancestors.

Once they were living on reservations (by 1854), the Ojibwas found their traditional way of life further attacked. There was not enough land to enable them to continue the old ways of hunting, fishing, and gathering food. The government expected them to become farmers, but the condition of the land, the short growing season, and the lack of machinery made farming very difficult, if not impossible.

A photograph taken at a Minnesota reservation school in the late 1800s. Under pressure from the American government, the Ojibwas gave up their traditional style of dress and went to school to learn English.

To make matters worse, through a policy called *allotment*, Indians lost much of their reservation land. Individual families were assigned small parcels of land, and much of the rest was sold to non-Indians. This process completely disregarded the cooperative spirit of Indian life. It also did not allow for any growth among the Indian people.

The Ojibwas were pressured to adopt the non-Indian way of life. They were given permanent housing and non-Indian clothing. The children were sent to reservation schools run by the government where the English language and history from an American point of view were taught. Some were sent far away to boarding schools. They were not allowed to speak their native language or observe any of their tribal customs. This policy was called *acculturation*, the process of adopting the ways of white society.

There was little work to be found on the reservations. Some of the Ojibwas went to work off the reservation in the lumber, mining, and railroad industries. A few were able to earn a living in more traditional ways by hunting and fishing. But for most Ojibwas, poverty was the result of all these changes.

THE BATTLE OF LEECH LAKE ▪ Each reservation had its own story of grievances against the American government. One of the places where the Ojibwas were most unhappy was the Leech Lake reservation in Minnesota. Thousands of acres of wild rice had been destroyed when the government built dams on Indian land. The government was behind in payments promised the people, and the Indians were not being treated respectfully by white law-enforcement officers. Sometimes they were arrested for very minor (or even imagined) reasons. Law officers would then take them 100 miles (160 kilometers) away to Duluth or St. Paul and force them to find their own way back.

In 1898 an incident involving an Ojibwa leader named Hole-in-the-Day sparked a deadly battle. Hole-in-the-Day had been arrested, but had escaped from police custody with the help of

his friends. The U.S. War Department responded by sending troops to the Leech Lake reservation. In this atmosphere of tension, a soldier's gun went off accidentally. Some of the Indians who were hiding in nearby woods returned fire, and a number of soldiers were killed.

The government sent still more troops. The situation might have become much worse, but fortunately both sides agreed to a peaceful settlement. Ojibwa leaders expressed regret for the deaths of the soldiers, and several Ojibwas went to jail. But the problems of poverty and injustice that had started the trouble remained.

This man, called Bug-ah-na-ge-shig, was the chief warrior in the Battle of Leech Lake.

Chapter Five

BETWEEN TWO WORLDS

In the early 1900s the Ojibwas struggled to survive on the reservations. Victimized by dishonest persons, they often received very little in return for their land, their forests, and their work.

A NEW DEAL ▪ In 1926 a private agency called the Institute for Government Research was asked by the U.S. Department of the Interior to examine conditions of Native Americans around the country. A panel of experts led by Lewis Meriam released their report in 1928. The Meriam Report described in detail the poverty of Indian people. It told of the poor diet, overcrowded housing, and widespread disease. There was little work available for adults, and the children were forced to go to schools where they worked like servants and were not allowed to practice their native culture in any way.

Some of the New Deal programs established by President Franklin D. Roosevelt in the 1930s helped to provide jobs for

*One of President Roosevelt's New Deal
programs in the 1930s established
nursery schools for Indian children.*

Ojibwas and other Indians. The programs supported physical improvements such as bridges, drainage systems, and roads and projects such as fish hatcheries, reforestation (the replanting of forests), and campgrounds.

With the outbreak of World War II, some Ojibwas were able to find work in war-related industries. Over 24,000 American Indians, including several hundred Ojibwas, served with the United States armed forces in the war. Despite decades of mistreatment, the Ojibwas proved themselves to be loyal American citizens.

After the war many Ojibwas went to live in cities around the country. They hoped to find jobs and opportunities to live a good life. But often they found that to be successful in a city they had to leave behind what was important to them as Anishinabe.

During the 1960s a number of organizations to promote Indian rights were formed. Across the nation, Native Americans worked to restore pride in their heritage.

Slowly, improvements were made. A landmark decision was handed down in 1983 when the case of two Ojibwa spearfisher-men arrested for fishing on land outside their reservation in northern Wisconsin reached a federal court. In what came to be known as the Voigt Decision, the court upheld the Indians' right to hunt and fish in traditional ways on any land that had belonged to their ancestors.

TODAY'S RESERVATIONS ■ Today, there are approximately 70,000 American Ojibwas, who live mostly on reservations in Michigan, Wisconsin, and Minnesota. In Canada, Ojibwas number approximately 130,000, living for the most part on reservations in Manitoba and Ontario. Each Ojibwa reservation has its own local governing council. Tribal leaders are elected by members of the tribe.

Ojibwa tribal members have a very special relationship with the American government. All members of Native American tribes are considered to be members of an independent nation (their tribe) as well as citizens of the United States.

Although the Ojibwas are spread out across a large geographic area, there are still many ties that bind them together. In 1990 there was a joint conference of Canadian and American

Ojibwas and Ottawas at the Sault Sainte Marie reservation. Such gatherings are important opportunities for members of Ojibwa bands to work together on issues that concern them.

Most Ojibwa leaders agree that one of the biggest concerns is education. Ojibwa children on the reservations are taught the basics, like reading, math, and science, just as non-Indian children are. In many places they are now also taught their native language and the history of their people.

Ojibwa children living in cities often have less support for their cultural heritage. That is why some cities now offer "immersion schools" for various ethnic groups, including Native Americans. In these schools students are immersed in, or surrounded by, people and classes that teach them who their people are and where they've come from as well as prepare them for the future. For Ojibwa children, wherever they live, learning to achieve a balance between the world of the past and the world of the future can be the most difficult and most important lesson.

Many other things besides education are important to today's Ojibwas. They are concerned about jobs for Indian people: There is a constant effort to attract more business to the reservations. They are also concerned about improving living conditions by providing health care and building better homes for reservation residents.

REVIVING THE OLD WAYS ▪ Beyond such social issues as education, jobs, and health care, there is one very important thing that binds many of today's Ojibwas together. It is pride in the teachings of the ancestors. There is an ever-increasing effort to carry on the old ways and teach them to the children.

Many of the cultural traditions described in earlier chapters are still alive today. Ojibwa people still gather and eat wild rice. They believe that it is a very special gift of the Great Spirit, and strongly resist non-Indian efforts to overharvest or destroy the watery fields where the rice grows.

Ojibwa people still carry on the tradition of producing maple sugar with the same spirit of thankfulness their ancestors had. Although aluminum and plastic equipment have largely replaced wooden spouts and birchbark containers, the process and the final product remain the same.

Ojibwas who participate in these and other traditional activities—including basketmaking and other crafts, hunting with bows and arrows, and ceremonial dances—say that these activities make them feel close to nature. Equally important, they feel close to their cultural roots.

A LIVING CULTURE ▪ As Ojibwa people work to revive their traditions, they try to find ways to interact positively with non-Indian society. They want to break down the stereotypes that many non-Indians have about them. They want to break through the invisibility that makes many non-Indians think that Native Americans are only people who lived a long time ago.

One of the ways that Ojibwas and other Native Americans show that they and their culture are alive is by holding *powwows*. Powwows are cultural and social gatherings during which various groups of Native Americans get together for singing, dancing, feasting, and other activities. Sometimes powwows are held to honor a particular group of Native Americans, such as veterans. Generally they are open to anyone who wants to participate.

*Above: Rice-gathering
by the Ojibwas in the
Great Lakes region
continues today.
Left: Very little has
changed in the way
the Ojibwas collect and
process maple sap.*

*Two members of an Ojibwa tribe prepare for a
ceremonial dance at a Canadian powwow in 1991.*

Powwows provide an opportunity for Ojibwas and other Indians to be with others of their heritage. They also provide an
opportunity for non-Indians to view the living culture of our
nation's first residents.

Another way in which the Ojibwas communicate with non-
Indians as they celebrate their culture is in the various museums
that they operate on reservation land. These museums are places
where both Indians and non-Indians can come to learn about the
past and present of Indian culture.

Newspapers and magazines published by Native Americans can also serve this function. The Ojibwas of the Lac Courte Oreilles reservation in Wisconsin operate a public-radio station. Besides offering music and information of interest to Ojibwas, it provides an outreach to surrounding non-Indian communities as well.

The Ojibwas manage a number of businesses on their reservations that are designed to draw non-Indians to their land. These include boat marinas and campgrounds, bingo parlors, and hotels. These and other recreational activities provide income for tribal members and an opportunity for the different cultures to interact.

■ ■ ■

Ojibwa people still live in their homeland territory, the northern Great Lakes region. As a tribe and as a people, they have survived their encounters with non-Indians. They were not destroyed as were some Native American groups, and they were not forced to move far from their homeland, as were many others.

Many Ojibwas still perform traditional activities and hold traditional beliefs. They also live in permanent homes, wear store-bought clothes, drive cars and pickup trucks, and work in many places of employment. As Americans and Ojibwas, they live in two worlds, continuing to seek ways to keep all things in balance and in harmony with nature.

AN OJIBWA STORY: WINEBOZHO LEARNS A LESSON

Among the many characters of Ojibwa legend, probably the greatest is Winebozho (sometimes known as Nanabush).

When the American scholar Henry Schoolcraft lived among the Ojibwas in the early 1800s, he wrote down the stories of Winebozho as told to him by Ojibwa people. The poet Henry Wadsworth Longfellow used these stories when he wrote the epic poem *Hiawatha*, although he gave the main character the name of a great Iroquois leader.

In many of the stories, Winebozho is searching for someone or something. In each of his searches, whether it be for his grandmother, his father, or an enemy, he learns many lessons. He learns about responsibility and happiness, about courage and foolishness.

Today Ojibwa storytellers still relate the adventures of Winebozho for both the education and entertainment of those who care to listen and learn.

The following is a story of a lesson learned by Winebozho as he searches for his grandmother. It is adapted from *The Mishomis Book* by Edward Benton Banai.

■ ■ ■

Winebozho was "first man," created by the Great Spirit. He was told that his grandmother lived across a great body of water. Finding the water, he tried to figure out how to get across it. He watched birds fly across the water, but he knew that he could not do that. He watched fish swim through the water, but he knew that he could not do that either, for the water was too vast.

Winebozho looked around some more. He saw that beavers cut down trees with their sharp teeth. That gave him an idea. He found a sharp stone and made an ax to cut down a tree. He dragged the tree to the water and climbed on. He thought he could float across on the log, but it kept rolling over and Winebozho kept falling off.

Winebozho thought some more. He thought about his brother the whale, who swam easily in the water without rolling over. He used his stone ax to shape the bottom of the log like the stomach of a whale, and to hollow out a seat for himself on top of the log.

He thought about the beaver's webbed feet and flat tail, which helped the beaver steer through the water. He used his ax to make a paddle that would help him steer his log-boat.

After several unsuccessful attempts to cross the water, Winebozho was finally ready. He had his log-boat and his paddle. He had some food and some water for the journey. He offered some tobacco in thanksgiving for these things and asked the spirits to help him complete his journey. He used the Sun and the Moon and the stars to guide him.

Winebozho had learned much. He had learned to use his animal brothers and sisters and the guidance of the spirits in the things around him. The Great Spirit was teaching him to live in harmony with all of Creation. Because he learned this lesson, he crossed the water safely and soon reached the wigwam of his grandmother, Nokomis.

IMPORTANT
DATES

1000 to
1400
Gradual migration of Ojibwas, Ottawas, and Potawatomis westward along the St. Lawrence River to the Great Lakes area.

1400s
Ojibwas settle along the shores of Lake Superior, establishing the village of Bowating near the present site of Sault Sainte Marie, and a village on Madeline Island in Chequamegon Bay.

1550s
Ojibwas become aware that fair-skinned strangers from far-off lands have arrived along the Atlantic coast.

1641
First contact between Ojibwas and Frenchmen at a Feast of the Dead ceremony hosted by Hurons on Georgian Bay, Ontario. Within weeks, French missionaries arrive at Bowating.

1659
French traders visit Ojibwa camps and begin trading directly with the Ojibwas rather than through Huron and Ottawa middlemen.

1662
Iroquois are driven from the eastern part of Ojibwa territory.

1698
Temporary suspension of the fur trade causes hardships for Lake Superior Ojibwas.

1736	Warfare between Ojibwas and Sioux breaks out in the upper Mississippi River valley in Wisconsin and Minnesota. The Sioux are gradually pushed westward.
1763	After the British defeat of the French in the French and Indian War, the Ojibwas are forced to trade with the British. Some Ojibwas participate in Pontiac's rebellion, an attempt to drive the British out.
1800s	Americans take control of the Great Lakes fur trade after winning the Revolutionary War and the War of 1812.
1854	By this time most Ojibwas in America and Canada have been forced to move to reservations within their old tribal territory.
1898	Battle of Leech Lake follows the sending of U.S. troops to the Leech Lake reservation after an Ojibwa leader resists arrest. Several soldiers are killed.
1928	Meriam Report describes the poverty conditions of Native Americans, including many Ojibwas.
1930s	New Deal programs bring some improvements to Ojibwa reservations.
1940s	During World War II many Ojibwas and other Native Americans serve in the U.S. armed forces and in support of America's war effort.
1983	The Voigt Decision states that Indian rights come before non-Indian rights in land use near reservations.
1990	Joint Conference between Canadian and American Ojibwas and Ottawas at Sault Sainte Marie.

GLOSSARY

acculturation. The process of changing a group's or person's culture to make it blend with another culture.

allotment. A piece of land assigned to a person. When reservations were broken up into allotments, much of the land not assigned to specific individuals was sold to non-Indians.

Anishinabe. Ojibwa word meaning "Original People" or "Original Man." This is what the Ojibwas traditionally call themselves.

coureurs de bois. French word meaning "runners of the woods." This was the name for the rugged, independent Frenchmen who traded with the Indians without licenses from the French government. They led a life filled with danger and adventure.

deadfall. A kind of trap used to catch and kill large animals. It is made with large pieces of wood arranged so that a heavy log falls on an animal's head or back after it enters the trap, killing it.

indigenous. Referring to the original or native population of a land. Indians are the indigenous people of North America.

makuk. Birchbark container made by the Ojibwas for storing many things, especially maple sugar and wild rice.

manido. A spirit. The plural of *manido* is *manidog*. The Ojibwas traditionally believed that all the things of nature have spirits. The Great Spirit is called Kitchi Manido.

Midewiwin. The special Medicine Society of the Ojibwa people. Only individuals who displayed a special relationship with the spirits were allowed to join. Members of the Midewiwin were healers who dealt with both physical and spiritual well-being.

pictographs. Pictures made by the Ojibwas that told the story of important events.

pitch. A sticky substance made by boiling the sap of certain evergreen trees. The Ojibwas used pitch to seal their canoes and other birchbark containers, making them waterproof.

portage. To carry canoes and supplies over land between rivers and lakes.

powwow. A cultural and ceremonial gathering of Native Americans.

puberty. The stage at which boys and girls experience physical and emotional changes that indicate that they are becoming men and women.

snare. A trap for catching and killing small animals and birds. It is made with a loop of string, and the prey is killed when its head is caught in the loop.

voyageurs. French word meaning "one who makes a voyage or journey." It was used to describe the traders who made long journeys between the French forts and trading centers of the eastern part of North America and the interior lands.

BIBLIOGRAPHY

*Books for children

*Benton-Banai, Edward. *The Mishomis Book*. St. Paul: Indian Country Press, 1979.

Billard, Jules B., ed. *The World of the American Indian*. Washington, D.C.: National Geographic Society, 1974.

Bjorklund, Karna L. *The Indians of Northeastern America*. New York: Dodd, Mead, 1969.

*Boyd, Catherine. *Falcon of the Forest: The Story of John Tanner's Life with the Indians*. Minneapolis: T.S. Denison, 1968.

*Broker, Ignatia. *Night Flying Woman: An Ojibway Narrative*. St. Paul: Minnesota Historical Society Press, 1983.

Brown, Craig, ed. *The Illustrated History of Canada*. Toronto: Lester and Orpen Dennys, 1987.

Carolissa Levi, Sister M. *Chippewa Indians of Yesterday and Today*. New York: Pageant Press, 1956.

Danziger, Edmund Jefferson, Jr. *The Chippewas of Lake Superior*. Norman: University of Oklahoma Press, 1978.

Densmore, Frances. *Chippewa Customs*. St. Paul: Minnesota Historical Society Press, 1979.

*Hofsinde, Robert (Gray-Wolf). *Indian Music Makers*. New York: William Morrow, 1967. Especially Chapter 6, "Indian Songs."

*Johnston, Basil. *By Canoe and Moccasin: Some Native Place Names of the Great Lakes*. Lakefield, Ont.: Waapoone Pub. & Promotion, 1986.

_____. *Ojibway Ceremonies*. Lincoln: University of Nebraska Press, 1982.

_____. *Ojibway Heritage*. New York: Columbia University Press, 1976.

Kubiak, William J. *Great Lakes Indians*. New York: Bonanza Books, 1970.

*Kvasnicka, Robert M. *Hole-in-the-Day*. Milwaukee: Raintree, 1990.

*O'Meara, Walter. *The Sioux Are Coming*. Boston: Houghton-Mifflin, 1971. Fiction.

Oxendine, Joseph B. *American Indian Sports Heritage*. Champaign, Ill.: Human Kinetics Books, 1988.

Ritzenthaler, Robert E. and Pat Ritzenthaler. *The Woodland Indians of the Western Great Lakes*. Milwaukee: Milwaukee Public Museum, 1970.

Seton, Julia M. *American Indian Arts*. New York: Ronald Press, 1962.

*Snake, Sam et al. *The Adventures of Nanabush: Ojibway Indian Stories*. Compiled by Emerson Coatsworth and David Coatsworth. New York: Atheneum, 1980.

*Spavin, Don. *Chippewa Dawn: Legends of an Indian People*. Bloomington: Minn.: Voyageur Press, 1977.

Waldman, Carl. *Atlas of the North American Indian*. New York: Facts on File, 1985.

Williams, Mentor L., ed. *Schoolcraft's Indian Legends*. East Lansing: Michigan State University Press, 1956.

INDEX